T
Patients
Who
Changed Me

SHAE
KOSCIELNIAK, RN

of the author's lived and professional experience. The content is intended for inspiration and reflection and is not a substitute for professional medical, legal, or therapeutic advice.

The inclusion of community-shared stories was done with gratitude and respect. All comments have been lightly edited for clarity and anonymity for the purpose of honoring the shared human experience of life, death, and healing. If you recognize your words and would like them credited, removed, or adjusted, please contact elevatewithshae@gmail.com.

For permissions, inquiries, or speaking requests, please contact: elevatewithshae@gmail.com

THE PATIENTS WHO CHANGED ME: LESSONS ON LIFE, LOVE, AND LETTING GO

A Collection of Hospice Stories & Reflections

Dear Reader,

If you've picked up this book, chances are... you've sat at someone's bedside.

Maybe it was your sister..

Maybe it was your mother.

Maybe it was your spouse.

Maybe it was a stranger who became your person in the quietest, most sacred hours.

You know what it's like to hold a hand and not know what to say.

You know what it feels like to whisper I love you and hope it reaches somewhere deep.

And maybe, like me, you've noticed the mystery in those final days. The way someone opens their eyes after days of silence, asks for root beer, or waits until everyone leaves the room to take their final breath.

These stories aren't just about death. They're about life. The kind of life that wakes you up, makes you pay attention, and reminds you what matters most.

As a hospice nurse, I didn't just care for people at the end.

I witnessed love. Regret. Healing. Humor. Peace.

And I started to realize... There is so much more going on than we can explain.

My hope is that as you read, you'll feel comforted, seen, and maybe even inspired to reflect on your own journey. Not just the losses, but the living.

You don't have to have all the answers.

You don't have to make everything make sense.

But I believe...deeply, that we're never alone in it all.

With love,

Shae

Contents:

Introduction

Part One: The Power of Connection

    1. Human Touch & the Need for Connection

    2. The Love That Never Leaves

    3. The Patients Who Became Family

Part 2: Life's Greatest Lessons

    4. Deathbed Regrets & What They Teach Us

    5. The Unexpected Teachers

    6. The Strength of the Human Spirit

Part 3: Signs, Synchronicities & the Spiritual Side of Hospice

    7. When Science Doesn't Have All the Answers

    8. Messages from Beyond, Signs, Synchronicities

    9. The Feeling of a Soul Leaving

    10. The Complexity of Faith at the End of Life

Closing Chapter: Living with Intention

    What Hospice Taught Me About Living

Compiled Community Stories

WELCOME TO MY WORLD.

Hi, I'm Shae. I've been in healthcare for almost twenty years, starting as a nursing assistant at 17, where I didn't quite know what I was stepping into but instinctively knew it was where I was meant to be. What began as a job quickly became my passion, and over the years, I've had the privilege of working with many people, especially the elderly, in a variety of settings: long-term care, home care, and hospice.

When I first started, I never expected that my career would take me on such an emotional and transformative journey. At 17, I helped with post-mortem care for the first time. It wasn't framed as an honor to the patient, it felt like a test, a trial of whether I had the fortitude to handle death. The other nursing assistants watched closely, waiting to see if I would falter. But I didn't. Even though I didn't fully understand life and death at the time, I felt an innate sense of calm. It just felt... right, normal. At that moment, I didn't shy away, and I wasn't afraid.

Looking back, I realize that moment was a kind of

initiation into my path. It was almost as if spirit was guiding me toward hospice, a calling I felt deep in my soul. After years of working as an LPN and RN, I knew it was time to try hospice care. When the opportunity arose, it felt like a natural next step.

Hospice has shaped not only my career but my personal growth. It's been in the quiet moments with patients, in hearing their stories and seeing their loved ones, that I've learned what truly matters in life. Through this, I began reassessing my own life, realizing that I was just going through the motions, pouring everything into patient care and leaving nothing for myself or my family. But as I witnessed people at the end of their lives, I realized the importance of living intentionally and finding balance in all areas of life.

As I share my story and the stories of those I've cared for, my goal is to offer insights and lessons that can help you live a more fulfilled, purposeful life. I'm not here to just talk about death. I'm here to talk about life. About how we can truly live in a way that honors ourselves and those around us.

This book is a reflection of my journey, my patients' journeys, and the wisdom I've gained along the way. I hope it serves as both a guide and an inspiration to help you navigate your own journey, no matter where you are on the path.

Reflection Prompts:

As you reflect on the stories and lessons in this book, I invite you to consider the following:

- Looking back on your life, do you ever feel like you were being guided toward a particular path, even if you didn't recognize it at the time?

- Have there been moments in your life where things fell into place in a way that felt serendipitous, as if you were meant to be in that moment or that place?

- Can you think of times where an unexpected experience, perhaps one you didn't fully understand, ended up shaping your future in ways you didn't foresee?

- How have the challenges or triumphs in your life led you to where you are today? What can you learn from them that can help guide you forward?

As you read through the stories shared here, I encourage you to reflect on your own life and consider what has shaped your path and where it may lead you next. Life often has a way of guiding us, even when we don't see it clearly at first.

PART ONE: THE POWER OF CONNECTION

1. Human Touch & the Need for Connection

More Than a Hug

Some patients leave a mark that stays with you forever, and Mary was one of those people for me.

I had recently returned to the field after about a year and a half in a desk role in quality assurance. As much as I appreciated the break from the emotional toll of hospice, I knew deep down I was meant to be back with people. To feel needed. To feel connected. Mary was one of the first patients I admitted when I came back, and somehow, that felt symbolic.

She was in her early 80s, living in an assisted living facility where she had stayed independently for years. She had initially moved in because of her husband, who had transitioned to memory care before eventually passing away. That space had held many phases of her life, and now, it was holding her final chapter.

Mary had advanced breast cancer. The tumor had grown to the outside of her skin, which meant I visited her three times a week to change her bandages. It was painful. Personal. Private. Something that was hard for her to allow anyone else to do. When not done gently or correctly, the dressings would stick, causing even more discomfort. Mondays were often rough, if it had drained through over the weekend and someone else had changed it, they'd sometimes forget the non-stick barrier. I'd be the one to gently manage the aftermath. We always pre-medicated before doing the dressing changes, but even with that, it was still a vulnerable, raw experience.

Despite her pain and the progression of her illness, Mary remained fiercely independent up until the last couple of months. But 2020 changed everything. The lockdowns. The testing. The isolation. Residents were mostly confined to their rooms. Families weren't allowed to visit. CNA safety checks and weekly (or sometimes twice-weekly) COVID swabs were the only touchpoints with the outside world for so long. It was a lonely time to be nearing the end of life.

Then came the nosebleeds.

It wouldn't stop. One day I arrived, blood poured for over an hour. Mary was overwhelmed and frightened. I stayed by her side, calmly doing what I could. Holding space. Reassuring. Cleaning. Monitoring. Finally, it slowed and stopped. I removed my face shield and leaned in to give her a hug.

She hugged me back like it was the very thing she'd been aching for, not just that day, but maybe for months.

With tear-filled eyes, she asked, "Are you even supposed to touch me like that?"

I smiled and said, "I've been up in your space this whole time. I think this is exactly what you needed."

"Thank you," she whispered. That moment felt like we both became connected forever. Sacred and healing in one embrace.

Mary and I connected in a way I don't think either of us expected. She was deeply spiritual and tapped into things that couldn't be explained with logic. She told me once that while living in California, she woke suddenly in the middle of the night with a terrible heaviness in her chest, only to find out later her father had died in a firefighting accident at that exact moment. She spoke of how she used to lie on a rock by the ocean, pondering life, feeling the pulse of the Earth and spirit around her.

And as my time in hospice was nearing its end, I let myself love her deeply. I knew I was about to transition into something "less." Less heavy, less intense, less emotional, but also less connected. So I leaned in. I allowed myself to care more, not less. I worried about her when I was off. I wanted her to have consistency, gentleness, and people who really saw her.

Telling her I was leaving hospice nine months later was heartbreaking. My patients were supposed to be saying goodbye to me, not the other way around. But in the way that only life, or maybe spirit can orchestrate, she passed just two days after our final visit.

I hugged her goodbye that last time, too.

I still have the Christmas decoration she had her daughter make for me in 2020 as a gift. I get to put it up every year and be reminded of her. Of us. Of what it means to really be with someone.

Our journey felt like more than patient and nurse. It was a mirror, her at the end of life, and me on the edge of something new. Her winding down, and me revving up. She helped me remember what matters: presence, connection, trust, intuition. And how human touch, offered with love and respect, can be a medicine all its own.

Maybe I wasn't just sent to her. Maybe she was sent to me, too.

Reflection Prompt

- Have you ever shared a moment with someone that felt divinely timed or orchestrated, like you were meant to cross paths at that exact stage of life?
- In what ways has touch, physical or emotional, brought healing or comfort into your life?
- When was the last time you let

yourself truly *connect* with someone, beyond roles, responsibilities, or expectations?

2. THE LOVE THAT NEVER LEAVES

Cora

We're not supposed to have favorite patients, but anyone who's ever worked in healthcare knows that's nearly impossible. Some people just etch themselves into your memory. Cora was one of those for me.

She had the kindest blue eyes, soft and knowing. Even when words had left her. By the time I met her, Cora was nonverbal. She was still mobile with some help at first, but slowly, her world became smaller as she transitioned into needing a Broda chair, mechanical lift transfers, and full care. I would visit, sit with her, play music, and trim her nails. Do all the "nurse things." The comfort checks, the medication management, and the gentle assessments. But more than that, I just *liked* being near her. There was a peace about her. A sweetness. I'd finish my charting beside her, sometimes feed her, help the aide with her baths or rounds.

Cora was on the younger side for end-stage dementia. Her husband had been her caregiver for years, navigating the slow, painful unraveling of the person he once knew. When her safety needs outgrew what he could provide, he made the heartbreaking decision to move her into a secure memory care unit.

He once told me about a day Cora became frightened and confused while they were driving home. In her panic, she began hitting him, and he had to pull over and call for help to get her home safely. He told me stories of standing in the doorway, blocking her from leaving the house when she tried to wander, believing she was somewhere else.

She was diagnosed in her early 60s and passed away in her late 70s. For nearly two decades, he loved her through the slow, daily, compounding loss.

And yet, when I met her, she was serene. The edges of her sharpness worn down by time, her confusion replaced by quiet presence. Her husband visited her often, always with gentleness.

There were whispers, hints that maybe he had started seeing someone new after Cora moved into the facility. Not in a way that felt scandalous or cruel. If anything, it felt… human. Honest. Real.

And I couldn't help but think, how could we fault someone for that?

Isn't love more layered than we give it credit for?

To care for someone as they slowly disappear before your eyes, year after year, and still show up with devotion. Isn't that love? And to also crave connection, touch, conversation, and to seek that elsewhere when the person you've loved no longer remembers your name... is that not love, too?

Love, I've found, isn't always linear. It changes shape. It adjusts, softens, expands. It doesn't have to fit inside one idea or promise. Maybe, just maybe, love makes room, for grief, for loyalty, for companionship, for the ache of needing to still *live* while watching someone you love slowly fade.

Years ago, there may have been a village to support someone through this. But today, that support is often missing. We are expected to do the unimaginable, alone. And yet somehow, people like Cora's husband rise to the occasion. Strong. Safe. Steady. And still human.

No one will ever replace Cora. I'm sure of that.
But I'm also sure, his love for her never left. It simply shifted forms. And that, too, is sacred.

"Love doesn't always look the way we imagined—but that doesn't make it any less real. True love expands, adapts, and remains—long after words are gone, long after roles have changed."

Reflection Prompts:

- Have you ever witnessed love that changed form but never disappeared? What did that look like?
- In what ways has your own definition of love,

loyalty, or partnership shifted over time?

- What expectations around caregiving, commitment, or "doing it right" might you be carrying that could be softened with compassion?
- Can love coexist with grief, and even joy, at the same time? What has your experience taught you?

3. THE PATIENTS WHO BECAME FAMILY

Evelyn

Have you ever felt like you were meant to meet someone? Like somehow, the universe put them in your path not just once, but over and over, until you couldn't ignore the deeper meaning behind it?

That's how I feel about Evelyn.

I first met her when I was 19, working as a nursing assistant in a neighboring small town. She was mostly independent then, just needed help with her medications, meals, and light housekeeping. Sweet as ever, part of a big, well-known Catholic family who had once owned the local bar for years. Everyone in town knew them.

A few years later, a new assisted living facility opened in her hometown. By then, I was fresh out of LPN school, working part-time there while also doing shifts in a transitional care unit. And guess who was there?

Evelyn. It felt like a full-circle moment.

Her care needs had increased, and eventually, she moved to the memory care unit. If anything, I loved her even more during that time. I've always had a soft spot for my dementia patients, their sweetness, their moments of clarity, their quiet grace. The challenge that comes with the not so sweet parts. There's a tenderness in those interactions that's hard to explain unless you've lived it.

Eventually, I moved on. Finished RN school, worked in metro assisted living settings, and then in home care. But the tug toward hospice was always there. Quiet, steady, persistent. It never went away.

Then one day, I got a call from my former LPN boss, who had moved on to a hospice agency and climbed the ranks there. She'd call me every time she had an opening, always with the same question:
"Ready to work for me yet?"

One day, she called and said, "I have a spot open, in your ideal territory. The one we used to work in." I said yes. And I'll never forget the moment I saw the caseload.

Evelyn was on it. After all those years... she was my patient again.
This time, in hospice.

She had been with me through nearly every chapter of my nursing journey. From CNA, to LPN, to RN, to hospice nurse. It felt surreal. Like something bigger had been orchestrating it all along. That kind of full-circle care doesn't just *happen.* Not by accident.

There have been many moments in my nursing career where I've felt that same sense of "meant to be." Like I was placed in a certain room, with a certain family, at a certain time. For a reason. Sometimes those moments were so profound, so perfectly aligned, that it felt less like coincidence and more like guidance.

I didn't grow up in a spiritual or religious household. We went to church on holidays, celebrated Christmas, and were taught that being a good, kind person was the most important thing. God was more of an idea than a presence. A "nice thought," rather than a certainty.

But hospice changed that for me.

Being with people at the end of life opened something in me. Call it God, call it Spirit, call it the universe, but whatever it is, I believe in it now. Not just because it sounds nice, but because I've *felt* it.

I've had moments where the right words came out of my mouth without me thinking, words that gave families chills or brought comfort they didn't know they needed. I've seen dementia patients completely lucid in the days before they passed, holding conversations after months of silence. I've seen patients talking to loved ones who had long since passed, eyes lit up, full of peace. I've felt the instant when a soul leaves the body, even when the heart is still beating for a few more seconds.

It's changed me.

Evelyn wasn't just a patient. She was a thread woven through the fabric of my entire career. A gentle reminder that love, connection, and purpose are always guiding us, even when we don't yet understand how or why.

She became family.
And I'm forever grateful.

"Some souls aren't just passing through—they're woven into the fabric of our journey, reminding us that love shows up exactly when and where it's meant to."

Reflection Prompts:

- Have you ever felt like you were "meant" to meet someone?
- What unexpected relationships have left an imprint on your heart?
- Have you ever crossed paths with someone again and again in unexpected ways?
- What do you think those repeated connections might be trying to show you?
- Who in your life felt like more than just a friend, patient, or acquaintance—someone who felt like family, even if they weren't?
- Have you ever experienced a moment that felt too meaningful to be coincidence? How did it shape your view of life, spirit, or purpose?

PART 2: LIFE'S GREATEST LESSONS

4. Deathbed Regrets & What They Teach Us

Do you ever find yourself holding onto regret?
A decision you made that haunts you.
A dream you never gave yourself permission to chase.
A mistake you buried deep instead of forgiving yourself for.

We all do this, to some degree. Carrying around guilt, resentment, or shame like armor. Thinking it protects us, but really, it just weighs us down.

As a hospice nurse, I've sat at the bedside of hundreds of dying people. Different walks of life. Different stories. And still… the regrets sound a lot alike.

The Weight We Carry

SHAE KOSCIELNIAK

Some people never seemed to let go of the pain.
Years of anger, blame, resentment. They wore it like a
heavy coat. It shaped their relationships, pushed people
away. And you could feel it in the room with them.

That general feeling that repels you from them. Sucks
all your energy while being around them.

Sometimes that anger stayed until the very end. Other
times, once the body began to fail, the fight drained
out. They didn't have the energy to stay angry. But that
didn't always mean peace.

Others turned all the blame inward, believing every bad
thing was their fault. They couldn't forgive themselves,
even when those around them had.

Common Regrets I've Heard

Some regrets are big. Some are quiet. But they echo
across lives:

- "I wish I had lived more for myself."
- "I wish I hadn't spent so much time worrying
  about what everyone else thought."
- "I wish I'd told her I was sorry before she was
  gone."
- "I wish I had been a better dad."
- "I wish I'd spent more time with my kids."
- "I wish I'd worn earplugs all those years at the
  factory."
- "I wish I hadn't waited until retirement to live and

now it's too late."
- "I wish I would have taken better care of my teeth."

Some of the saddest ones come from people who *planned* to live, later.

They had the camper in the driveway. The road trip route picked out. The travel list was written. But the diagnosis came first.

The Truth Behind the Regret

Regret doesn't mean you did everything wrong.
It means you're human.

We all feel pain, we all make mistakes.
We grieve, we forgive, we learn, we grow. That's life.

But if there's one thing I've learned sitting bedside with the dying, it's this:
You don't have to wait until you're dying to choose a different way to live.

What Their Regrets Taught Me

These stories opened me up.
They made me reflect. Deeply.

What am I holding onto that isn't mine anymore?
Where am I staying small because I'm afraid of what people will think?
Have I told the people I love what they mean to me, *enough* times?

So many people die wishing they had done things differently.
But some…
Some die with peace in their hearts.

And those are the ones I study closely.
They forgave.
They laughed.
They prioritized presence over perfection.
They made hard decisions earlier than they were ready.
They loved even when it hurt.

Don't Wait

Maybe you have time left.
Maybe you're young or healthy or still "figuring it out."
But time has a funny way of running out before we expect it to.

What if you gave yourself permission to let go of old pain today?
What if you said the apology, or forgave the person, or booked the damn trip?
What if you didn't need a diagnosis to wake up to your life?

You are not too late.
You are still here.

And that means you still get to choose.

Reflection Prompts:

- If you had one year left, how would you spend it?
- What small changes can you make today to align with what truly matters?

5. THE UNEXPECTED TEACHERS

The Camper Guy

There are patients you never forget, not because they were warm or graceful or easy to love, but because they opened you up in ways you didn't expect. He was one of those patients. Unfiltered. Unpredictable. And despite everything... unforgettable.

He was known as "The Camper Guy" to all my friends who've heard his stories, due to the fact that he had an RV that caused quite a few dramatic sagas in the course of my caring for him!

The Kind of House You Don't Set Down Your Backpack

I met him in his home, it was definitely one of those "keep your shoes on" houses. You don't take off your coat. You don't set anything on the floor. You just... adapt. Backpack stays on your back. He lived alone, surrounded by rusted campers and vans in the yard, claiming the city had repossessed some just to spite him. So he just bought more. Out of spite.

Inside, he shared the space with a very old poodle named Bingo, rotting food, fruit flies, and piles of dishes. It was chaos. It was gross.

He was still of sound mind, so unable to be deemed self neglectful by state laws.

He let me into his world through one layer of grime and stories at a time. Stories that didn't always line up. He was a man who had once owned this house proudly. A man who had once had a family, had a purpose, had structure. But life had slowly unraveled around him and maybe within him.

Maggots and Denial

There are moments in nursing that live with you forever. The first time I saw live maggots in a wound was with him.

I was crouched beside his leg doing wound care when I saw them. Little, wriggling translucent things. I blinked hard. It didn't feel real. But it was.

I was *very* thankful to be wearing a face mask at this time so he didn't see my full facial expression.

"Bob, I think you have maggots in your wound."

He scoffed. "No! There's no damn bugs in there. You're crazy."

I pointed. "Um, well somethings moving in your leg. Look."

He peered down, still skeptical. "Well what the hell, how would they have gotten in there?!" Eventually he went to the ER. Driving himself, maggots and all. He returned home a couple days later, maggot-free but still surrounded by the same conditions that birthed them.

It wasn't just the wound that refused to heal, it was his life.

The Stories We Tell Ourselves

Bob told me often, "If I didn't have bad luck, I wouldn't have any luck at all." A phrase he clung to like a badge of honor, like a reason for every heartbreak and betrayal.

He trusted everyone and got burned by almost all of them. But the ones he trusted were those who I've always been told not to trust... Hitchhikers who offered sex and then stole his meds. Roommates who left coffee cans filled with feces. A woman who robbed him of his camera collection. His daughter, who he swore stole his change from his motorhome.

And yet, he kept letting people in. Over and over. As if some part of him still hoped someone would stay and not leave a mess behind.

I kept telling him he needed to stop saying "if I didn't have bad luck, I wouldn't have any luck at all," because clearly it was a self fulfilling prophecy, manifesting in his life, proven time and time again.

Losing and Leaving

Bob lost his home not with a bang, but with a taped

eviction notice. I saw it before he did, and had to deliver the notice to him. Paired with a missed virtual court hearing. Reverse mortgage. COVID confusion. Missed payments. Miscommunication. And before he knew it, or maybe just as he expected, he was packing up his life into a van and motorhome, moving from campsite to extended-stay hotel to VA assistance housing.

Through it all, he remained oddly upbeat, or at least determined. He bought a new van with cash while living in subsidized housing. Got into a car accident with no insurance. Fell for a $97 fake Costco generator scam. Insisted the world was just out to get him. Really it seemed on the outside, he just never learned.

Broken Bonds

His relationships with his children were splintered, complicated, and unresolved. One son never spoke to him again after Bob "mistakenly" called his son's ex "looking for a good time." He hadn't talked to his daughter in over a year, a Facebook fight followed by texting the wrong number for months, convinced she was ignoring him.

He removed them all from his will. From his emergency contacts. From the narrative of who he thought cared for him. And yet... he still talked about them.

This was the thing about Bob, he was an open wound wrapped in thick layers of deflection and denial. But he bled anyway.

The Soft Cracks in the Armor

As the end approached, the cracks widened.

I could sense it was the end. He wasn't on hospice, just trying to fight the good fight, keep on keepn' on. I started to have the thoughts of, "Is he going to be alive when I get there?" Those thoughts are usually a good indicator things are coming to an end. Part of that "death sense" that comes along with hospice experience. His legs swelled. His oxygen needs increased. He got a catheter he couldn't manage. His dog Bingo passed away.

"I don't think Bingo feels pain," he once said. "I accidentally rolled over him with my chair, and he didn't even yelp."

Somehow, that line gutted me more than anything.

And yet… even at the end, there were glimmers. He made friends in his apartment building. Elderly women who fussed over him. Made him food, checked on him.

But the chaos still followed him as well, even into his 90s. Somehow the same type of people found him at every stage in life. Other residents asking him to borrow vodka until their next social security payment or for an oxycodone until their next refill date.

He died in the hospital. His daughter made it to the bedside for his last 24hrs.

What Bob Taught Me

Bob taught me things I didn't expect to learn. Things that I carry still.

- *The illusion of control:* You can try to order life, but sometimes it remains messy and sometimes, it's the mess that makes it real.

- *The need for connection:* Even in his most paranoid, stubborn moments, Bob wanted to be seen. He needed to be heard, even if he didn't know how to ask.

- *The harm of old stories:* "If I didn't have bad luck..." That belief became a prophecy. His identity. It's what he looked for and what he found. I told him, "You have to stop saying that." I wish he had.

- *The dignity of choice:* He lived how he wanted, even if it looked tragic from the outside. The system tried to intervene, but he was competent, and his choices were his own.

- *The duality of people:* Bob was equal parts angry and generous. Bitter and hopeful. Lonely and loved. A contradiction wrapped in a dirty recliner and stubborn resolve.

I don't know if Bob ever found peace. I hope he did.

But in some strange way, through the chaos, the infections, the arguments, the stories...Bob gave me a gift. He reminded me that even the most unpredictable, difficult, wild patients can be sacred mirrors. Teachers in disguise. Even if he drove me nuts at times.

He was, in all his flawed glory... an unexpected teacher.

He is also the reason why I know of a nudist campground in Minnesota...

"Everyone you meet is fighting a battle you know nothing about. Be kind. Always."

— Robin Williams

Reflection Prompts:

- Have you ever learned something profound from someone you least expected?
  What was the lesson, and how did it impact your perspective?
- Bob lived in what many would call chaos, yet he still invited connection.
  How do you hold space for complexity in others? In yourself?
- Think of someone in your life who challenged you deeply.
  What might that experience have taught you about compassion, patience, or boundaries?
- Bob struggled with trust and disappointment but kept opening the door.
  Where in your life do you notice a similar pattern? either in giving too much or holding back too tightly?
- Despite his hardships, Bob kept trying to live life on his terms.
  What does "living life on your terms" mean to you right now?

6. THE STRENGTH OF THE HUMAN SPIRIT

Mack

Some of the most profound connections I've had with patients in hospice came from the most unlikely souls. Mack was one of those souls.

Mack had been diagnosed with a brain tumor years prior. No further testing. No aggressive treatment. Just living life, on his terms. He was living at home alone, fully independent, smoking cigarettes, drinking, smoking weed, and binge-watching sci-fi documentaries about wormholes and aliens. He didn't believe in heaven, but he believed in UFOs.

I was his nurse for two years. Every week, I'd visit and often stay far longer than scheduled, just listening to his stories. And boy could he talk!

He was a Vietnam veteran, my favorite kind of patient. Gruff and rough around the edges, but under all that armor was the little boy who was sent to war too young.

The protector underneath all the tough exterior, all wrapped up as a beautiful complicated mess at times.

Another Vietnam vet explained to me once how different their war was. He had served in the war and then later became a social worker for the VA. He explained that they didn't go as units, they went as individuals. They arrived as the new guy, always the outsider, always alone. Cycling in and out of the unit, leading to lack of trust, loneliness, fear. That loneliness clung to them even after they returned. And when they came home, many were met not with honor, but with silence and shame.

That war broke a lot of people. Some managed to claw their way forward, but many stayed trapped; battling chronic disease, addiction, anger, suicide, and the slow ache of loneliness.

Mack had seen it all. He told me stories of nearly taking his own life in the aftermath of his divorce. Memories of him rocking back and forth on his bed holding a gun, battling between ending his life or his ex wife's. His love for his kids saved him.

He still carried deep resentment and guilt, but he also carried love. So much love.

He joked that dying was just "taking a dirt nap." He wanted to be buried with his cellphone, a pack of cigarettes, and a lighter "just in case he woke up underground." His humor was dark, but I think it masked a very real fear: that this life might be all there is.

He was the only patient whose funeral I attended. The one who cracked me wide open.

I still remember the poem his friend read. Mack wrote it himself after he returned home from Vietnam. It was messy, beautiful, raw. Just like Mack.

Near the end, Mack's brain tumor began to progress. He declined fast, like falling off the edge of a cliff after years of plateau. His daughter, balancing life as a working mom, moved in those last weeks to care for him. She was exhausted, pulled between being present for her young kids and her dying father.

Mack lingered in transition for weeks. He'd go without food or water for days, and then suddenly wake up, ask for fast food, smoke a cigarette, and go back to sleep. I still really don't understand how someone can have regular periods of apnea but yet can wake up with enough lung strength to inhale a cigarette.

We thought "this is it" more than once. I remember being at his bedside when he stopped breathing for a full minute. The air changed. Something swept through the room. An energy, a feeling that couldn't be ignored. Think goose bumps on steroids that you feel through the deepest part of you. His daughter and I felt it, we both cried. Then he took another breath and came back.

I wonder what he was holding on to. Was it fear? Regret? The unshakable belief that there was nothing else after this life?

In those final weeks, I visited daily. Assessing comfort, supporting the family, monitoring progression. I would wash him up, complete the bed bath, turn and reposition. Something that was hard for him to allow his daughter to do or any others for that matter. After cleaning up the water basin, towels, and bedside, I dumped out the water. The used water I poured out had turned gray, without a logical explanation. He was in bed, not getting up, not getting dirty. And it felt as if I was washing away his pain, cleansing what he couldn't forgive in himself. It was more than caregiving. It was a spiritual exchange. A ritual. An act of love.

After Mack died, I'd sometimes smell cigarette smoke in my car and feel his presence, like he was riding shotgun, still keeping watch.

Honestly, even now as I'm writing his story, I feel him. I almost gave him a different name and felt the little whisper, "don't you dare name me that."

His daughter messaged me a year later after he passed. She still felt his hand in hers sometimes.

Jack taught me that the human spirit is vast, complex, and enduring. He was angry, funny, messy, brilliant, skeptical, kind, and broken, all at once. But his spirit? It held on. It transformed me. And maybe, in his own way, he was transformed too.

I am so grateful for the time I spent with him. The life lessons he gifted me by just being him are something I will cherish forever. Thank you Mack!

"The human spirit is stronger than anything that can happen to it." — C.C. Scott

Reflection Prompts

- Have you ever met someone whose story challenged your beliefs about life or death?
- What have you seen or experienced that made you question what happens after we die?
- Have you ever experienced connection with someone who has passed? A smell, an embrace, a presence?
- Is there a part of yourself that still needs forgiveness or release?
- How do you want to be remembered—what spirit or presence would you want leave behind?

PART THREE: SIGNS, SYNCHRONICITIES & THE SPIRITUAL SIDE OF HOSPICE

7. When Science Doesn't Have All the Answers

The Rally

She had been mostly unresponsive for weeks. A 102-year-old woman, quiet, still, declining slowly like a candle burning down. No pain meds needed. She was just... slipping. Peaceful, really. We had all accepted that it was coming. Her body knew. Her time was near.

Most of her family had already passed, she had outlived just about everyone. There wasn't a lot of people around. She'd had a long life, and now it was just a matter of waiting.

Then one day, out of nowhere, she woke up.

I'm talking clear-eyed, alert, and straight-up spicy. She looked at one of the nurses who had just walked in and said, "What are you trying to do? Kill me?" with that signature sass like she hadn't been in a near-comatose state for weeks.

And then, of course, she asked for a root beer. That had been her thing for years. Barely ate much else, just root beer, all day long. It was her simple pleasure, her comfort, her ritual.

So we gave her one. She drank it. She smiled. She sat up and chatted, laughing with staff, reminiscing. It was like watching someone come back to life. Not in a dramatic movie-scene kind of way, but in a quiet, familiar, soul-shaking kind of way.

It didn't last long. A few hours, maybe. Then she slipped back into sleep. A week later, she died peacefully.

There's no real explanation for it. In hospice we call it "the rally" or "the surge." Sometimes people have a final burst of energy, clarity, presence, before they go. It's not every time, but when it happens, it stops you in your tracks.

It doesn't make sense. No one can fully explain it. It doesn't match the science. Her body was shutting down. She had no fluid intake. She should've been too weak. But somehow, something inside of her chose to wake up, connect, say goodbye in her own way.

And I think... that's kind of the point. Not everything is meant to be explained. Not everything about death or life fits into tidy little boxes.

There are moments where you just have to be there. Feel it. Witness it.

This was one of those moments. It made me believe even more that we are more than just our bodies. That something else takes over in those final days. Something sacred. Something we don't have words for.

And I've learned that when those moments come, the best thing we can do is be still. Stay close. Let the mystery do what it does.

"Not everything that counts can be counted, and not everything that can be counted counts." — Albert Einstein

Reflection prompts:

- Have you ever witnessed something that didn't make sense but felt deeply real?
- What are the small simple moments or rituals, like root beer for her, that have brought comfort to someone you love?
- What do you think happens in the space between life and death?

8. MESSAGES FROM BEYOND, SIGNS, SYNCHRONICITIES

There have been so many moments in my life that, at first, just seemed like strange coincidences. Those flickers of déjà vu I used to brush off or forget. Looking back now, I know they were more than that. They were whispers from spirit, nudges, signs, and guidance that I often ignored or didn't yet know how to interpret.

Working in hospice over the years changed that. Being present during a soul's final moments, witnessing the shift in the room as someone passes, the peace, the stillness, the beauty that words struggle to describe. It awakened something in me. I began to notice how often patients would talk to loved ones who had already passed, or speak of "going home," or preparing for a trip, or packing a suitcase. These experiences stayed with me. They rooted themselves in my spirit, slowly waking me up to a deeper knowing that I could no longer dismiss.

I never completely denied the idea of something beyond this life. But I also didn't actively claim faith, God, religion, or spirit. I figured something likely existed, but I didn't spend much time thinking about it or living from that place. But over time, after standing beside so many people at the edge of life, I came to embody a new truth: spirit is real, and we are not alone.

These lessons, the messages, the synchronicities, the unmistakable sense that our loved ones are still with us, have become the clearest thing for me to share. The stories that follow are just a few of those sacred moments.

Jewel

My Auntie Jewel passed away on my mom's birthday in 2021. She had been a little fragile in her later years, living with chronic health issues. When she got COVID, she was too scared to seek medical care. By the time she asked for help, it was too late.

Jewel was a retired nurse herself. I grew up hearing stories about how she would hold the hands of dying residents in the nursing home after her shift, just so they wouldn't have to be alone. She was the family nurse too. Showing up when anyone needed care. She moved in with her sister-in-law during her cancer diagnosis, helped hold the family together, and stayed up through the night with her dying brother so others could rest. She lived a life of service, almost to a fault. She even suffered from "broken heart syndrome," where emotional stress literally damages the heart.

When her health took a turn, her kids flew to Texas from Minnesota to bring her home. She refused to go to the hospital unless they could be with her. So, they made the road trip, her CPAP machine plugged into the car adapter so she could breathe. She was admitted to the hospital her son worked at, then later transferred. Eventually, she was ventilated and isolated. Her daughter sat in the parking lot, just to be near her.

As the end neared, the family began discussing how to say goodbye. My mom struggled with whether to make the three-hour drive. COVID fears were still high, and Jewel was sedated and on a ventilator. I told my mom that maybe, if Jewel was really transitioning, she could connect with her just as powerfully from home, through words, prayers, or even thoughts if that's what she chose.

After Jewel passed, strange things started happening. My mom felt her presence in the house. Jewel's Willow Tree angel figurine was found turned around in a locked display hutch. Puzzle pieces went missing. Clocks changed. My mom, who's usually skeptical, began greeting the signs with a simple, "Hi, Jewel." Accepting that it was her sister, still showing up in love.

A few months later, my mom, Jewel's first granddaughter (who she helped raise), and I planned a lunch date. As I was getting ready, doing my makeup and hair, I thought, *Jewel would've loved to be here for this.* So I invited her. I said, in my mind, *Jewel, would you like to come to lunch with us? If you're with us, could you send me a sign of a jewel so I know you're there?*

Ten minutes later, my mom arrived to pick me up. She came inside, said hi to my daughter, and excitedly handed her something.

"Laina! Look what I saved for you! I found this jewel in the soap, it's so pretty, isn't it?"

I stood frozen in the kitchen, the fridge door still open, jaw hanging. Full-body chills. That goosebump rush that says, *no way, but also... of course.* I was stunned, but also filled with joy and awe.

I told my mom the story in the car. I was a little nervous she wouldn't believe me, but how could I not share it?

I had expected maybe the waitress at lunch would be named Jewel. Instead, she showed up early. She heard the invitation.

Love you, Auntie.

Harper
Every year, I take a trip with close friends. We've been to Mexico, Florida, Sedona... In December 2023, four couples went together to an all-inclusive resort, sunshine, relaxation, and drinks flowing. One of my friends on the trip was Harper, another hospice nurse from a small town in northern Minnesota.

On our first day, we got settled at the beach bar. Harper stepped into the designated smoking area nearby and struck up a conversation with a woman from California. Like always, the conversation quickly turned to "Where are you from?" The classic vacation icebreaker.

Harper mentioned her tiny Minnesota town, population under 1,000. The woman's eyes lit up. She said, "My grandma just passed away and she lived in that town! She was 100."

Turns out, Harper had cared for her grandma in hospice.

The woman shared the story with the bride. They took it as a sign. Grandma was sending her blessing. There were tears, laughter, and that undeniable feeling that Grandma was still very much a part of the celebration.

Life is just so cool sometimes.

Eagles

My mother-in-law passed away young, just 57. Dementia at 52. A brain tumor found six months before she died. She loved her children deeply, and most of all, her grandbabies.

After she passed, I felt more connected to her in spirit than I had in her last few years alive. I invited her to our family gatherings in my thoughts. I'd feel her with us.

One summer Saturday, the day of my father-in-law's birthday party, I found myself thinking about her on my morning walk. The sun was out, the air was light, and I thought, *Debbie would've loved this day.* So I invited her to join us.

Then I added, *If you'll be with us today, could you send me a sign of an eagle to know that you're here?*

Just a few minutes later, eyes down as I walked, I noticed a large shadow glide across the ground. I looked up. An eagle soared overhead, close, wide-winged, unmistakable.

Full-body chills.

I felt her with me all day. Like the air was lighter, the joy deeper, the connection stronger.

Miss you, Debbie.

Reflection Prompts:

- Have you ever received a sign from spirit/universe/god or a loved one who passed?
- What do you believe happens after we die?

9. THE FEELING OF A SOUL LEAVING

There's something impossible to fully explain about the moment someone takes their last breath. The room shifts. Something changes, not just physically, but energetically. I've felt it. I've witnessed it. And while I've been present for several last breaths, no two are exactly the same.

Sometimes death comes quietly. Sometimes it's triggered by a larger stimulus. One particular experience still sits heavy with me.

It was a weekend. I was on call and sent out to admit a new patient at an assisted living facility. When I arrived, it was immediately clear the weekend staff didn't really know what was going on. No one seemed to have been checking on him. I found him slumped in his recliner, unresponsive, rapid wet-sounding breaths, irregular pulse, high fever. He was soaked in sweat and urine. Alone. No family there. No DNR signed. Just me, a phone line to the on-call doctor, and a distant cousin listed as the emergency contact.

One look, and I knew the end was near. But what

haunted me most was knowing he might die right there in that chair, unclean, seemingly forgotten. I couldn't let that happen. But I also couldn't move him on my own, he was over 250 pounds and completely unresponsive. His bed was in the other room.

I called the physician, got a stat order in for a Hoyer lift and comfort meds, but they wouldn't arrive for another four hours. I found facility staff, explained what was happening, and asked them to keep an eye on him. I had to step away for another visit before the lift arrived.

When I returned, the lift had just been delivered. I called his cousin again and explained the situation, that moving him might stress his body to the point that it could stop his heart. The family contact and the doctor gave me a verbal ok: do not resuscitate if he passed during the transfer.

With one staff member assisting me, we got the sling under him and carefully lifted him from the recliner. We placed him into the bed. Gave him a moment to settle, then began cleaning him, removing his soiled clothing, gently turning him to cleanse his body.

It was during the second roll that I felt it.

The shift.

The moment.

I knew.

I had been sensing death was already close. It had been there, inching closer with each moment. I had prepared the aide, the family, myself. I had talked to the patient throughout, honoring him even though he couldn't respond. And just then, with his cousin on the phone, his final breath came.

And it felt final.

It's hard to explain, the absence of breath, yes, but also the absence of spirit. Of energy. A knowing that the person, their essence, is no longer inside their body.

And in almost every death I've witnessed, there is peace after the death.

I've not been present for trauma or emergency deaths. Only the ones that were anticipated, expected, planned for. There is something sacred in that. I've worked alongside nurses who could predict time of death within hours. One could even smell death three days beforehand. I didn't believe it until I experienced it myself. A distinct smell in the last 12–24 hours of life. Not every nurse can detect it. Some say it's sweet. Some think your crazy when you talk about it. But it's there. Another reminder that some things can't be explained by science or our five senses.

Impending death has a feeling. A presence. A sense. A deep awareness. And no it's not doom. It just *is.*

It feels like the closing of a loop. A cycle completing. Exactly how it was meant to be.

In those final minutes, there's often a calm anticipation. A peaceful energy shift. It doesn't feel lonely. It feels like Spirit is near. Supporting the person passing. Supporting those present. Supporting those of us there to serve.

I've felt myself guided in those moments, words flowing through me that I knew weren't mine. I didn't consciously think the words in my head and then say them, they just came out. Along with the goose bumps when its delivery landed. Actions and instincts rising up like I was being led. Often I'd never met the person before, yet somehow there I was, midwifing their soul out of their body with sacredness, presence, and care. While personally feeling naturally calm and at ease in the midst of such heavy moments.

Grief and death are not the same. Grief comes after, and it's for the living. Death, though, can be its own kind of peace.

Reflection Prompts:

- What emotions come up when you think about death?
- How can we shift our fear of death into something more peaceful?

10. THE COMPLEXITY OF FAITH AT THE END OF LIFE

They were one of the loveliest couples I'd ever had the honor of knowing. Devoted Christians, deeply planted in their church and community. He had been a teacher, a principal, and later worked maintenance in "retirement." She had been the heart of their church choir, both as director and organist. Together, they built a life of service, family, and faith.

Their days followed familiar rhythms, even in their final years. Every afternoon, they'd go to the same local pizza place for lunch. It became more than a meal. It became a measure of their strength, a way to gauge if they could still make it out into the world together. They built a community wherever they went.

Margaret was the first to go. Her final years were challenging in a slow slipping away. She spoke often, almost every visit, about being ready to "go home" to the Lord. There was peace in her words, a knowing. But her body lingered longer than her spirit wanted to. Dementia crept in quietly. There were falls, hospitalizations, and eventually a diagnosis of a luekemia. Even when she was mostly bed-bound, barely eating, barely awake, treatments continued. Including ambulance rides to the hospital for transfusions.

Her family wrestled with electing hospice care. They feared the hospice nurse wouldn't be Christian, and they believed every possible intervention needed to be exhausted before they could release her to God's will. I struggled internally. I saw the exhaustion in her tiny frame. I witnessed how treatments robbed her of the very peace she had spent years yearning for. But being of service meant meeting them where they were, not where I wished they would be.

Faith is complex. Sometimes it's trusting that letting go is an act of faith itself. Other times, it's clinging to every last breath as a measure of devotion. I had to learn again that honoring someone's path means holding space for their struggle, even when it doesn't align with my own beliefs about life, death, and surrender.

Margaret passed quietly one afternoon. Her long wait to go "home" finally fulfilled.

Walter, her husband, lived another year. He was ninety-seven, still tending his gardens, still sharing canna bulbs and catalpa seeds with anyone willing to plant them. Even in his grief, he found ways to serve, to connect, to teach. His faith was woven into everything he did. He spent time daily with his caregiver, studying the Bible with her until she eventually joined his church.

And yet, under the surface of his devoted life, Walter carried a grief few knew about. One snowy day long ago, he had been in a car accident. Two teenagers lost their lives; he survived. Decades later, the sorrow was still fresh. He confided in me one day, "I killed two kids," his voice thick with shame.

Despite a life of kindness, love, and service, Walter struggled to believe he was truly forgiven. He spoke often of sin, redemption, and unworthiness, as though the stain on his soul could never be washed away.

His garden bloomed brightly every summer, a testament to the life and love he shared. Yet inside, a part of him remained trapped in winter.

Faith at the end of life is not always clean or simple. Even the most devoted believers can wrestle with forgiveness, of themselves, of others, of the inevitable surrender that death requires. Service, I learned through Walter and Margaret, isn't about fixing or forcing or correcting. It's about showing up with love, empathy, and compassion even when I don't understand. Even when my heart aches with the tension of wanting a different ending.

I still drive by their house sometimes. The gardens are quiet now. But the seeds they planted, in their community and in me, are still growing.

Caring for others at the end of their lives often invites us into a sacred tension—where our own beliefs, hopes, and understanding of faith might differ from theirs. True service, however, is not about correcting, convincing, or steering someone toward what we think is best.

It's about standing with them exactly as they are.

It's about surrendering our own need to "fix" and choosing instead to love, witness, and hold space, even when their choices and struggles feel difficult for us to understand.

The complexity of faith is not a flaw; it's part of the raw beauty of being human. In the end, grace is not something we earn by getting it all "right." It's something we are worthy of, simply by existing.

"The beginning of love is the will to let those we love be perfectly themselves, the resolution not to twist them to fit our own image."

— Thomas Merton

Reflection Prompts:

- Where in my life have I found it difficult to accept someone's choices or beliefs?
- How can I practice deeper empathy and presence, even when I don't fully agree or understand?

- What does surrender mean to me in the context of faith, caregiving, or service?
- How do I personally define "grace"? How can I offer it more freely—to others, and to myself?

CLOSING CHAPTER: LIVING WITH INTENTION

WHAT HOSPICE TAUGHT ME ABOUT LIVING

When I started hospice nursing at 26, I *thought* I knew what I was getting into, but I really had no idea.

Those first few years were a blur. I was fully immersed in hospice work that I genuinely loved, while also navigating early motherhood. I was pregnant with my daughter during that time, and there was something so symbolic about it all, bringing life into the world while caring for those at the end of theirs.

It felt sacred.
Beautiful and heavy.
Joy and grief, creation and surrender, all swirling together.

I moved fast through those early years, juggling babies, work, marriage, figuring out my 20s, and holding space for families in some of the most tender moments of their lives. The weight of it didn't settle right away. I didn't have time to stop and feel it.

But by year four, I started to.

I felt it more.
I *saw* it more.
I opened to it.

The emotions, the existential questions, the midlife reflection hit me like a wave:
What is life really about?
Am I happy?
Am I living the life I want or just surviving the one I ended up in?

I felt this tension, like I was doing so much good, but also carrying a quiet ache that I couldn't name. A feeling of being trapped, overwhelmed, responsible for everything and everyone... and yet completely disconnected from *me*.

I think that's a common experience for nurses.

We're so used to morphing into whatever version of ourselves is most helpful in the moment. I can become whatever type of nurse my patient needed, blunt and firm, soft and nurturing, light and funny, or just neutral and professional. I can read a room and shape-shift in seconds.

But that habit doesn't turn off when the shift ends.
Over time, that conditioning seeps into every part of life.
You forget who *you* are when you're not performing for someone else.

Eventually, the resentment creeps in. The exhaustion. The loss of self.

So I stepped away. I took a "soft" nursing job. Gave myself some space to breathe.

And in that space, I started making sense of it all.

I reflected on the hundreds of patients I'd cared for at the end of their lives, the hands I'd held, the grieving families I'd hugged. The regrets I'd heard again and again:

"I wish I had done more for *me*."
"I wish I hadn't wasted so much time worrying what people thought."
"I wish I had made amends sooner."
"I wish I had taken that trip while I still could."

I've had patients with a camper in the driveway that they never got to take across the country because a stroke came first.

I don't think people mean to put life on hold. I think we're all just doing our best.
But witnessing so much death has gifted me something rare: *clarity.*

I've seen and felt spirit.
I've grieved the loss of patients I came to love.
I've lost people in my personal life, too.

And I've also lived moments that made my chest burst wide open in awe, laughing, crying, heart pounding, thinking:

"Wow. I can't believe this is my life."

All those years of hearing people's stories gave me a mirror.
They helped me examine *my* life.
What felt aligned, what didn't.
Where I felt peace, where I felt pain.
And what I was willing to change.

I realized I didn't choose all the pieces of my life, some just happened because I followed what society laid out. But if it wasn't making me feel alive, or fulfilled *me*, then maybe it was time to rewrite some of it.

I didn't want to be afraid of change anymore.
I didn't want to numb my way through life or live for everyone else's expectations.
I wanted joy. Connection. Creativity. Laughter. Presence.

I wanted to sit next to my husband and cry happy tears as the helicopter lifted off the ground.
I wanted to be at my kids' games, fully present, not distracted by all the noise.

Maybe life *isn't* supposed to be so serious.
Maybe we're here to feel good.

To love.
To connect.
To create.
To laugh, play, rest, and really *listen.*

What if building a meaningful life is as simple as doing

more of what makes you feel *alive*, even if it looks different than what others expect?

I've learned that I'm really good at loving people, exactly as they are, whether they're messy and raw or living their best selves.

I've learned how to forgive.
How to let go.
How to evolve.
How to be soft and strong at the same time.

And I've learned that everyone changes. Everything does.
The only constant is change itself.

Hospice taught me that we don't get forever.
But we *do* get to choose what we do with the time we have.

So I'm choosing to live with intention.
To live a life that feels good on the inside—not just one that looks good on the outside.
To be more *me* and trust that it's more than enough.

Reflection Prompts:

- If you were dying tomorrow, what would you wish for those you love that are still living? Would you wish for them to go live and love and play and experience?
- What changes can you make now to ensure you're living fully?

COMMUNITY COMMENTS:

The stories we carry don't end with us—they echo. These words from members of my community remind us that death is often full of mystery, timing, and quiet connection. These stories are real. And they are sacred.

This includes selected anonymous comments and experiences shared publicly on social media. For the purpose of further connecting with others, knowing you are not alone in your experiences, loss and grief. All comments have been lightly edited for clarity and anonymity. If you recognize your words and would like them credited, removed, or adjusted, please contact elevatewithshae@gmail.com.

THE KNOWING: WHEN THEY SEEMED TO SENSE IT WAS TIME

"He wasn't dying. His health was stable, and he was going about life as usual. Two weeks before his birthday, he started saying, 'I'm not going to make it.' A week later, he mentioned getting a cat. Days after that, a tragic accident took him. The day before his memorial, a stranger called about a cat I'd once considered adopting. It was in the same town as a family member, who brought it to me. That cat became my comfort—marked with a heart-shaped spot."

"They told the nurse they were going to head home for the night. A minute before they would have left, their loved one passed. It was as if they waited until the moment they felt safe to go."

"After three weeks in the hospital, they insisted on going home—even though it was against medical advice. Just hours after arriving, they passed peacefully. They knew it was time."

"He waited until everyone was on their way. One person left the room briefly. One was still traveling. And then he passed. He had even asked someone to take a specific week off work—it ended up being the week of his service."

THEY WAITED FOR THE RIGHT MOMENT OR THE RIGHT PERSON

"One family member drove across the country on a gut feeling. The moment they arrived, the person passed. There were just too many perfect alignments for it to be coincidence."

"He waited until every child and their partner had made it. Once the last person was safe and present, he let go."

"The moment I walked into the house, the call came. I know they didn't want me to witness the moment."

"We were outside talking with a nurse. Suddenly, we were called inside—it was time. Somehow, my partner just *knew*. The person passing always had a quiet trust in him, even without recognition."

"She somehow knew her grandson was coming, even without phones to notify her. He made it, and shortly after, she passed."

SIGNS, VISITS &
THE UNSEEN

"I asked for a sign after they passed. Later, when I was home alone thinking about them, a bottle flew across the room. I couldn't help but laugh."

"I wished they were with me on a beautiful day. A white feather floated into my hand. I didn't take it as coincidence."

"After sitting hospice, strange things began—like the car radio turning on by itself, playing songs that held meaning. Then one day, it just stopped."

"We always joked about the number 4 and a favorite season. I asked for a sign, and someone randomly brought up the number during conversation. It made me smile."

"I find dimes in odd places. The TV changes to sports when I'm watching something else. It feels like a familiar presence still playing tricks."

"Dragonflies swarmed a tree near me—dozens of them. It felt like a hello."

"Alone in the house, I heard my name clearly from down the hall. No one was there."

THE UNEXPLAINABLE KNOWING

"I knew someone had passed about 20 minutes before the call came, even though we hadn't spoken in ages."

"After waking from a long coma, I remembered every person who visited—and what they said. Everyone was shocked I knew."

"I thought someone had to be there at the end. But she passed quietly at night, when no one was around. It was so her—never wanting to cause a fuss."

WAITING UNTIL THEY ARE ALONE

"Both of us left the bedside for just a minute—one for medicine, one to the nurse's station. Our loved ones passed while we were gone. We believe they waited for privacy."

"Everyone had gone to bed. I woke up suddenly—just moments after they passed. I think they waited for the quiet."

"We stepped away for just a few minutes. When we returned, it had happened."

"After days at the bedside, I felt a sudden calm and knew it was time to go home. She passed 20 minutes later."

"That morning, she got up, used the restroom, and asked for ice cream. She passed peacefully later that day while we stepped out. I'm just glad we had that sweet moment."

"He didn't want to be alone—but still, he passed in the 45 seconds I stepped out. I hope he knew I was nearby."

"I stayed with her every day for a month. The one night I wasn't there, she passed. I wonder if she chose that timing for my sake."

"Every single one—four grandparents, another elder, and a parent—waited until the room was empty. A hospice nurse once told me that's more common than we think."

"She had been unconscious for days but waited until we stepped outside. She just knew."

"I joked with him before stepping away for five minutes. I suddenly heard laughter in my head—when I returned, he was gone."

"She was always one to want space. Of course she waited until everyone finally left her alone."

"They hear and feel everything. Leaving us is the hardest part. But they try to ease our grief. They take our love with them, and we keep theirs here."

"They don't want the final memory to be painful. They know what we can and can't handle."

"The care team told us, 'She did it her way.' And I believe that. She waited for the right moment."

Printed in Dunstable, United Kingdom

63503161R00047